Carsten Schneider

Operational IT Implementation Management. Transition from IT Projects to IT Operations

GRIN Publishing

Bibliographic information published by the German National Library:

The German National Library lists this publication in the National Bibliography; detailed bibliographic data are available on the Internet at http://dnb.dnb.de .

Imprint:

Copyright © 2014 GRIN Verlag GmbH
Print and binding: Books on Demand GmbH, Norderstedt Germany
ISBN: 978-3-656-94325-9

This book at GRIN:

http://www.grin.com/en/e-book/296318/operational-it-implementation-management-transition-from-it-projects-to

GRIN - Your knowledge has value

Since its foundation in 1998, GRIN has specialized in publishing academic texts by students, college teachers and other academics as e-book and printed book. The website www.grin.com is an ideal platform for presenting term papers, final papers, scientific essays, dissertations and specialist books.

Visit us on the internet:

http://www.grin.com/

http://www.facebook.com/grincom

http://www.twitter.com/grin_com

Operational IT implementation management

Transition from IT projects to IT operations

Course of studies:	International Bachelor of Business Administration
Organisation:	Hessische Berufsakademie
Semester:	WS 2013/2014
Student:	Carsten Schneider
Place & Date:	Berlin, 08.02.2014
Keywords:	IT projects, IT operation, transition, IT projects vs. IT operation, handover, ITIL, PMI, IT service lifecycle, project lifecycle, flexibility vs. stability, frameworks, IT organisation

Table of contents

List of abbreviations

ASL	Application services library
CRM	Customer relationship management
ELS	Early life support
GUI	Graphical user interface
HP	Hewlett-Packard
HR	Human resource management
ISPL	Information services procurement library
IT	Information technology
IPMA	International project management association
IP	Internet protocol
ITIL	IT infrastructure library
LAN	Local area network
Mgmt	Management
OS	Operating system
PC	Personal computer
PLC	Project life cycle
PMI	Project management institute
SLA	Service level agreement
SDLC	Software development life cycle
WAN	Wide area networks

List of figures

List of tables

Appendix

1 Introduction

IT operation in large companies is mostly faced with two major challenges. On the one hand IT should provide reliable, secure and user friendly services like email, desktop-services and accounting or CRM systems. On the other hand IT operation should be very adaptable and able to follow business development without any delay. Due to globalisation and increasing competition, business and consequently IT operations are forced to adapt to current market conditions. For example, the VW Golf III had been produced for ten years before it was replaced by the Golf IV. In 2012, the VW Golf VI was replaced by the successor model after only five years.

An increasing number of changes have to be made in a shorter time. Nearly every major change is implemented within a project organisation. As per data from Gartner and other research agencies, in 2008 more than $2.7 trillion were spent on IT and software projects worldwide. This massive amount demonstrates the importance of IT projects for the company's business. Endeavours in the form of a project are considered to be faster and more flexible than normal company organization structure. In particular, large changes in big companies are difficult to implement without formal project organisation.

The IT project organizes and executes large changes with a certain aim, within a fixed period of time and with an allocated budget. After the project is finished, the IT project organisation is dissolved and responsibility for the project's results is handed over to the operational and organisational structure of the company, if necessary. The transition from IT project to operations during the entire project lifetime, needs special attention and management, especially when facing resource problems or other major delays. Once the IT project is finished, IT operation assumes responsibility for running costs, maintenance and trouble-free operation within the IT system landscape. The connection between IT projects and IT operations, from outset to conclusion of a project, are the subject of this thesis.

In particular, answers will be sought for the following questions:

- What is IT operation and what are the biggest challenges in IT operations?
- What are the special characteristics of IT and IT projects?
- What kind of relations between IT projects and IT operations exist?
- What kind of services are provided by IT operations during an IT project?

The first part of this thesis describes the general characteristics of IT operations. After an overview of the key processes the chapter takes a detailed look at the current challenges IT operations is facing. The next part describes the theory of project management by considering the different lifecycle phases. Additionally, focus is placed on special characteristics of IT projects in general and in particular within the project phases. In this context, development, testing and deployment of the project`s outcome must be given special consideration.

Chapter 4 deals with the interfaces between IT operations and IT project based on preceding chapters. In addition to organisational aspects, common transition processes were introduced. A further focal point is the interface between IT operations and IT projects. Possible IT operations activities during the project phase and within the transition processes are described and listed. The thesis ends with a conclusion and provides alternative notions that may improve the cooperation between IT operations, projects and transition processes.

2 IT operations

This chapter describes responsibilities and significance of IT operations. It starts with a deeper look into some chosen operational processes, emphasizing current challenges in this area. After a detailed look at some chosen operational processes, the current challenges in this area will be emphasized. In this context, the term Information Technology (IT) refers to everything related to technology that is used to store, process and distribute information and other contents.[1] One subarea is analysis and evaluation of information, another subarea is control and automation of business processes. An additional focus of IT is the entire area of communication, with wireless service products, internet and machine to machine communication.

2.1 Definition of IT Operations

The definition of IT operations differs throughout the industry, where vendors and individual organizations often create their own custom definitions. IT operations coordinate and carry out the activities and processes required to deliver and manage IT services on agreed levels for business user and customer. This is normally defined within a service level agreement (SLA). A service level agreement describes the characteristics of IT services, documents service level targets, and specifies the responsibility of the IT operations and the customer responsibility.[2] IT operations is therefore responsible for the ongoing management of the technology that is used to deliver and support IT services. Well designed and implemented processes will be of little value if the day to day operation of those services is not properly conducted, controlled and managed. The improvement of IT operations requires a monitored day to day activity. Furthermore, data has to be collected and systematically analysed.[3] Besides monitoring and controlling, the range of activities usually includes management, deployment, distribution, implementation, installation, verification, execution and maintenance.

---

[1] Cf. (Royal Academy of Engineering and the British Computer Society, 2004), p. 7
[2] Cf. (The Stationery Office - A, 2011), p. 106
[3] Cf. (The Stationery Office, 2007), p. 13

IT Operation performs these daily activities and takes care of the availability of the IT infrastructure, such as email or CRM systems. This includes all of the facilities, software, networks and hardware. The operation staff keeps the implemented IT systems running in the defined quality. Logistics activities like installing desktop systems, networks or populating server racks are also part of IT operations, as are installing software and monitoring, controlling and maintaining the existing IT systems. The required skill set varies widely for each of these different tasks. The various activities have to be organized in order to keep the IT complexity under control and to ensure that staff shortage or unexpected events can be handled professionally, without major impact. In every organisation the right structure is extremely important for efficient operation. Figure 1 shows an example of department organization structure, based on technologies and tasks.

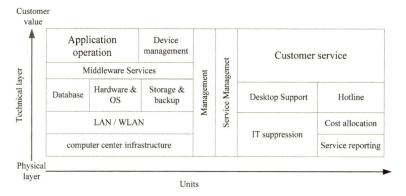

Figure 1: Example organization structure IT operations, based on Bock, 2010, p8

On the one hand the organisational structure based on different technology layers, provides an optimal support of individual IT components, but - on the other hand it offers only limited customer-focused support. Because of its key role for the business, IT departments transform themselves from a technology-driven to a customer-oriented IT service provider.[4] Against this background, common processes and procedures, policies, roles,

---

[4] Cf. (Bock, 2010), p. 10

responsibilities, terminology, best practices and standards have to be defined for reliable IT operations. For this purpose, IT management approaches like the Information Services Procurement Library (ISPL), the Application Services Library (ASL) or the IT Infrastructure Library (ITIL) have been developed. ITIL provides a framework of best practice guidance for IT management, which has become the most widely used and accepted approach to IT Management in the world. It provides a universally accepted framework for establishing a set of integrated processes for delivering high quality IT services.[5] The ITIL Framework in version 3 is based on the idea that delivering IT services is of vital value to the business and a strategic goal of the IT organisation. An IT service in ITIL is defined as every service that uses a combination of information technology, people and processes to support the customer's business processes, directly or indirectly. Hereby, a customer can be within the same organisation or within an external organisation.[6] In addition to the concept for IT operations, ITIL also provides concepts for strategy, design, transition and continual improvement of IT services. These five core publications build a lifecycle that a uses hub-and-spoke design as shown in Figure 2: service strategy at the hub, and service design, transition and operation as the revolving lifecycle stages or 'spokes'. Continual service improvement surrounds and supports all stages of the service lifecycle. The life cycle phases are cross connected to each other so that every phase impacts another. Therefore the IT Operation is greatly influenced by upstream processes and decisions.

---

[5] Cf. (itSMF International), p. 103
[6] Cf. (The Stationery Office - C, 2011), p. 13

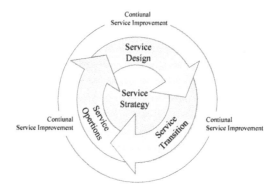

Figure 2: ITIL life cycle, based on Ebel, 2008, p. 36

2.2   Core processes for IT operations

In general, a process is a structured set of activities designed to accomplish a specific objective. A process takes one or more defined inputs and transforms them into defined outputs. Within IT, operations processes are used to organise the technology driven approaches to an activity based method. Processes can improve the productivity within an organisation and make activities repeatable, comparable and measurable. Measurable process characteristics are performance, cost, quality and quantities, the specific process results, and if a customer that uses the process directly or indirectly.[7] Once defined, the process should be documented and controlled. Every process is initiated by a trigger which might be an event or a specific request. The output of one process can be the input for one or more additional processes. For this reason, process often generates process chains within process landscapes, as shown in Figure 3.

Figure 3: Simple ITIL process chain, based on Ebel, 2008, p. 468

---

[7] Cf. (The Stationery Office - C, 2011), p. 21

Special significance for the work of IT operations are the interference suppression processes, like incident and problem management, as well as processes that change the existing IT environment, such as change, release and deployment management.

2.2.1 Event management

Event management deals with any detectable or discernible occurrence that has significance for the IT environment. Events are typically recognized through notifications from the IT infrastructure, by a user or a monitoring tool. Nearly every IT item or IT process that can be automated needs to be controlled. Virtually all those kinds of IT items and IT processes fall within the scope of event management. Some IT components are included because they have to be available 24x7 like a network router, whilst other components change their status frequently and hence specific actions are required. For example, memory usage of a server needs to be monitored.[8] Furthermore, environmental conditions, software licence monitoring and IT security are in the scope of event management, as well as normal activities like monitoring the processor load of an application server. Monitoring and event management are closely related but have a slightly different nature. Monitoring covers every occurrence, while event management includes only occurrences that are specifically generated to be monitored. In other words, monitoring is about handling a stream of events, while event management deals only with specified events.

Effective IT Operation depends on knowing the initial state, combined with a good understanding of the target status of the IT environment. Every event and related impact has to be evaluated in order to notice deviations, incidents and possible risks for IT services or IT environments. After evaluation, the event records will either be closed or trigger new processes. [9]

2.2.2 Incident and problem management

Each incident is triggered by an event like a system error log entry, a message from a user or by the technical staff itself. An example of incidents might be lost network connectivity of a client or reported software failures due to source code issues. Both incidents have

---

[8] Cf. (The Stationery Office - C, 2011), p. 58
[9] Cf. (Ebel, 2008), p. 458

different root causes and require different actions in order to restore the IT service. The purpose of the incident management process is to restore normal service operation as soon as possible, after any kind of IT service interruption or other deviations from the SLA. The goal is to reduce the impact on the delivered IT service and therefore to minimize the impact on business operations. This approach ensures the best possible levels of service quality and availability. An incident is defined as an unplanned interruption of an IT service or a reduction in the quality of an IT service. Besides that, a failure of components that have not directly impacted the business service, like backup systems or failure of one disk from a mirror set, is also considered an incident.[10] IT operations have to take all appropriate means to restore normal operations as quickly as possible, with the least possible impact on the business and the user, at a cost-effective price. The incident management process is responsible for managing the lifecycle of all incidents until the failure has been remedied. It ensures the use of standardized methods and procedures for efficient and prompt response, documentation, ongoing management and reporting of incidents.[11] The root cause analysis may be a part of the process, however only when it is definitely necessary to restore the IT service and no workaround is available.

Unlike the incident management process, which is focused on restoring the IT service as soon as possible, the problem management process handles the unknown root cause of one or more incidents.[12] The problem management process seeks to minimize the adverse impact of incidents and problems on the business that are caused by unknown errors within the IT Infrastructure. In order to achieve this, the problem management uses two basic approaches. The reactive problem management identifies the root cause of incidents, documents and communicates known errors and initiates changes to improve or correct the situation. The proactive problem management identifies and solves problems and known errors before further incidents related to them can occur again. As an ongoing process, the proactive problem management tries to find patterns and trends within the incident, event and change records that may indicate the presence of underlying errors in the infrastructure.

---

[10] Cf. (The Stationery Office - C, 2011), p. 72
[11] Cf. (The Stationery Office - C, 2011), p. 72
[12] Cf. (The Stationery Office - C, 2011), p. 98

2.2.3   Change management

The Change management process takes care of all changes that could have an effect on IT services, enabling beneficial changes to be made with minimal disruption. A change is the addition, modification or removal of any item that has a direct relationship to the IT environment.[13] There are plenty of reasons for changes, for example the implementation of an IT service, like a new CRM system or new desktop clients, the installation of a software patch on a server- or the assignment of new permissions for a user. The change management process has to evaluate every change for risk, impact to the IT and business, resource requirements and especially authorization. Changes generally differ in their size, in relation to the needed budget, time and other resources, as they differ a lot in their impact on IT and business. The exchange of a network router is a relatively small change concerning budget and time, but it can affect every IT service that depends on this component and therefore every business process that uses these IT services. It is essential to maintain the required balance between the need for change, and the impact of that change. The great majority of all incidents that occur are based on unauthorized changes.[14] The correct authorisations, completed in time and at the right time, from the competent organizational units are one of the biggest challenges of change management. Even if a change request was processed correctly, the risk for the IT environment is still high. In particular, changes which are requested for the first time, are a major challenge for IT operation.

2.2.4   Request fulfilment

To handle the large number of changes and to maintain user and customer satisfaction the request fulfilment process has been introduced. Password changes by users, movement of a desktop PC from one room to another or the executions of a defined report are typical demands in the daily work within an organisation. Request fulfilment handles a defined set of service requests, changes and other actives that frequently repeat, typically with low risk, low cost and small scale. These characteristics prefer those requests to be handled

---

[13] Cf. (The Stationery Office - B, 2011), p. 61
[14] Cf. (Ebel, 2008), p. 376

separately. Otherwise, processes like change management get congested and obstructed by business as usual tasks. [15]

2.3   Challenges in IT operation

In addition to day to day operation and the observance of service level agreements, IT operations have to meet several challenges. Those challenges are usually associated with the company organization structure and complexity of vertical range of manufacture.

Flexibility

In light of enhanced global competition, the non IT departments face a growing demand on short-term provisioning of IT services. Regarding delivery time, product development, decision-making and other customer requests the departments have to be more flexible and react faster than in the past. IT operations have to keep pace with the rapid changes that occur in most IT environments today. The pace of change has been accelerated by the increasing range of possible IT services, like virtualization, IP-based storage, etc. But this increased range is opposite to the quest of operational stability.[16] In IT, it is very difficult to predict the effects of making small changes in software and other components and therefore to anticipate possible failures.[17]

Customer orientation

IT organisation teams are often based on the technological structure, like database or network operations. This kind of separation by technology provides a higher degree of technical expertise. The focus on one technology or one product guarantees the formation and development of expert knowhow. However for those kinds of organizational units, it is often difficult to understand the business as a whole and therefore the business requirements in detail. Technical subunits often lack the information to understand which system supports which business process. From the team's viewpoint, every system or

---

[15] Cf. (The Stationery Office - C, 2011), p. 86
[16] Cf. (Bock, 2010), p. 8
[17] Cf. (Royal Academy of Engineering and the British Computer Society, 2004), p. 16

service with the same SLA has an identical criticality.[18] For example, a management reporting system has the same SLA as the company's online shop. In the worst case, both services fail at the same time and IT operations focusses on the reporting system, resulting in major sales losses due to the online shop outage. On the other hand, non-IT units aren't able to understand the vertical range of manufacture of IT, which makes it too complex to change anything within the IT environment.

Costs

The budget spent on IT worldwide is estimated at US $3.5 trillion and it is currently growing at 5% per year. Approximately 75% of this expenditure are recurring costs, used to "keep the lights on" in the IT-operations.[19] Hence, IT budget is always under pressure of cost savings. Once an IT service is implemented it is expected to run with the assumed budget. Very few organisations plan effectively for the cost of ongoing management of IT services. It is not easy to quantify the cost of a project, but it is just as difficult to quantify what the service will cost after years of operation.[20] In particular, design flaws or unforeseen requirements make it difficult to obtain funding during the operations stage. These kinds of problems often occur months after start-up.

Efficiency

IT operations is challenged by the task of structuring the workflows and processes more efficiently and reliably. This includes organisational aspects, technology and personnel, in order to meet the business expectations. Efficiency in this case basically means, "doing more with less", maintaining or improving the quality of IT services while constantly reducing the cost of these services.[21] This approach is reinforced and justified by the ability of the IT operations staff. The IT staff is able to automate processes and to take advantage of synergies between IT services.

---

[18] Cf. (Bock, 2010), p. 8
[19] Cf. http://omtco.eu/wp-content/, p. 2
[20] Cf. (The Stationery Office - C, 2011), p. 35
[21] Cf. http://www.teamquest.com/pdfs/, p. 5

On the one hand, it is expected that IT operations get more efficient in the day to day business, on the other hand, it is difficult to obtain additional funding for tools or actions aimed at improving the efficiency of operations. The customer expects that these costs would have been built into the cost of the service from the start. Once an IT service has been successfully launched, and been operational for a period of time, the service is taken for granted and any action to optimize it is perceived as fixing a service that is not broken.
[22]

Clear distinction of tasks and responsibilities

In projects and as part of business processes, IT operations can be involved in several tasks. Here it may occur, that task characteristics differ widely from the core competency of IT operations. A clear distinction of tasks and responsibilities is necessary to reduce difficulties arising from suboptimal task sharing.

The current separation between operation al staff and the teams involved in IT projects was originally deliberate to prevent collusion and to avoid potential security risks. The different duties of IT operations and IT projects could be a source of rivalry and political manoeuvring within an enterprise.[23] A clear organisational structure considering virtual teams and matrix organisation, is essential to guide staff and management decisions. This separation and distinction has to apply to personnel and for individual tasks as well. The basis for cooperation between IT projects and IT operations is often simple resource planning, based on available headcount. For example: new IT services often consist of standard software with an individual part of source code. User roles, GUI views and reports may be configured by the standard software. Normally, configuration of IT components is part of the responsibility of IT operations. If these tasks are not included in the scope of the project, for example due to the fact that these activities are part of standard performance for the view of the project, it could result in resource-related conflicts or a lack of resources.

---

[22] Cf. (The Stationery Office - C, 2011), p. 36
[23] Cf. (The Stationery Office - C, 2011), p. 233

If operational staff is involved in business processes, this could rapidly lead to comprehension difficulties and misinterpretations. The distribution of tasks and transition points, between business units as customers, and IT operations as supplier might be complex. Even when IT operations is considered as customer-oriented, it cannot fulfil customer requirements proactively by itself. For example: although a billing run starts every month at the same point in time, IT operations should not start the process proactively in order to support the business in the best way. The business has to give a clear order instead.

3   IT projects

The vast majority of all changes are performed within projects. This section focuses on the theory of projects and project management in general. After an overview of different project phases, special characteristic of IT projects will be discussed.

3.1   Project characteristics

Similar to terms like "Strategy" or "Vision", there is no unique definition for the term project, but a set of definitions from different organisations, educational institutions or scientific publications. The Project Management Institute (PMI) defines a project as "... a temporary endeavour undertaken to create a unique product, service, or result."[24] The International Project Management Association (IPMA) describes a project as "... a temporary form of organisation for a relatively unique, short to medium term process that involves several organisational units in particular."[25] And the Oxford dictionary says that a project is "a collaborative enterprise, frequently involving research or design that is carefully planned to achieve a particular aim".[26] In general, a project has a set of primary characteristics - it has a specific goal, it is temporary and therefore limited, it is unique and produces a unique outcome. In addition, a project is also described as complex and

---

[24] Cf. (Project Management Institute, 2004), p. 5 f.
[25] Cf. (pma PROJEKT MANAGEMENT AUSTRIA, 2009), p. 7
[26] Cf. https://oxforddictionaries.com/definition/

interdisciplinary due to the fact that it affects many different areas of responsibility in one organisation. The following is a list of main project characteristics in detail.

Goal

In general, projects are goal-oriented endeavours. The bedrock of a project is a certain aim and the entire venture depends on that aim and is linked to it. The goal of the project, not the project itself, is the prime motivation. Project objectives define target status at the end of the project, which are necessary for the achievement of planned benefits. Project objectives have to be formulated operationally, regarding both the desired quality and quantity. Objectives can be broken down into main objectives (targets) and additional objectives.[27] Functional project boundaries can be defined more clearly by defining non-objectives, if required. Clear objectives should meet the following characteristics, also known as the SMART criteria:[28]

Specific The goal must be well defined and focused, and should not be general. The more precisely the goal is described, the more likely it ends up where it should. Therefore, it is necessary to describe the goal as precisely as possible.

"Sales obtain 50 new billion dollar corporate clients in Europe with project A" is more meaningful than "Generate more revenue with the project A"

Measurable The goal must contain concrete criteria for measuring progress. Objectives should include several numeric or descriptive measures which define quantity, quality, time and cost via indicators like milestones dates, budget, created lines of code, etc. to measure the project outcomes along the way. These measurable criteria are prerequisites for controlling the project and for comparing if the goal has been successfully met at the end of the project.

---

[27] Cf. (pma PROJEKT MANAGEMENT AUSTRIA, 2009), p. 28
[28] Cf. (Phillips, 2010), p. 20

14

Achievable	The project's goal should be achievable, considering the resources, cost, and the time required versus what's available for the project organization. This means that the goals are neither out of reach, nor below standard performance but simple, realistic and attainable. It's important to be aware of the contributing factors, which will help to reach - or not reach - the expected outcome. Therefore, the goal's achievability had a strong relationship to the project scope and to the balance of time and budget. Comparative values, experiences and estimated efforts are the basis of the assessment of attainability.
Relevant	The goal of the project should be the right endeavour at the right time. It should support the further primary needs of the institution, provide opportunities for the institution, or solve problems. Relevant goals are based on the current conditions and realities of the environment. A goal can be specified, measurable, attainable, and time-bound, but lacks relevance. Therefore it is important to choose the right number of goals that are significant for the institution.
Time-bound	The goal should be grounded within a certain date. Like the measurement aspect, having time bound goals is another way to mark off progress and realize success. A time-bound goal is intended to establish a sense of urgency. A commitment to a specific date helps the project to focus the efforts on archiving the goal before the due date.

Temporary

Every project has a definite beginning and a definitive end. The beginning takes place when the project goal is defined and the formal initiating starts. When the goals have been achieved, the project ends. Similarly, when it becomes clear that the project objectives will or cannot be met, the objectives are obsolete, or the need for the project no longer exists, the project is terminated.[29] Temporary does not mean short in duration, projects can last for many years. One project is never part of the on-going efforts of an organisation. In contrast,

---

[29] Cf. (Project Management Institute, 2004), p. 5 f.

15

the time limit does not general apply to the result or output created by a project. For example, a project to build a train station or a public airport will create a result expected to last many years. Often the opportunity or market window is temporary – some projects have a limited time frame in which to produce their product or service.[30]

Unique

Projects have to create unique outcomes, like products, services or other results. Uniqueness is one characteristic of project deliverables. Therefore, the project deliverables have to be seen as a whole. Even if a construction company has built hundreds of standard one-family houses, but each individual building is unique – different owner, different location, different season and so on. Depending on the perspective, more or less parameters are distinctive. The presence of repetitive elements does not change the fundamental uniqueness of the project.[31]

The characteristics temporary, goal orientated and unique are general for a project. However, a term that is also often stressed when projects are defined, is scope. Depending on the type of project being implemented, and the nature of the organization, the project's scope contains authorization, objectives, product or service description, constraints, acceptance criteria, deliverables, exclusions and assumptions regarding the project.[32] All this information is held in the project scope statement, as an output of the project initiation. The project scope defines what is included and what is excluded within a project and the terms and conditions under which the project takes place.

3.2 Project management and project life cycle

Project management is the application of knowledge, skills, techniques and tools to execute projects effectively and efficiently. To execute a project effectively and efficiently, comprehensive leadership throughout the initiating, planning, executing, monitoring,

---

[30] Cf. (Project Management Institute, 2004), p 5 f.
[31] Cf. (Project Management Institute, 2004), p. 5 f.
[32] Cf. (Phillips, 2010), p. 20

controlling, and closing phase is needed.[33] The primary challenge of project management is to achieve the project goals and objectives under present constraints.[34] Like many human undertakings, projects need to be performed and delivered under certain restrictions. The primary constraints are scope, time and budget, which are closely related to each other. Time and budget are normally limited resources, as scope, presenting the objective demands and requirements of a project, is more susceptible to increasing contents. The relationship between these constraints is depicted as an equilateral triangle, as shown in Figure 4. Each side represents a constraint. This illustrates that scope, time and budget are firmly connected together. One constraint cannot be changed without affecting the others.

Figure 4: Project triangle, own illustration

Therefore, scope, time and budget are competing demands. For example, if scope is extended or a new deliverable is added to the project, time and money needs to increase equivalently. The sides of the triangle must be in balance with one another for the project to be successful.[35] The interior of the triangle stands for quality and/or customer satisfaction and therefore scope, time and budget have a direct impact. Often the triple constraint issues are the core of the most crucial decisions about a project.[36] Therefore, the discipline of Project Management is about providing the tools, methods and techniques that enable the project team to organize their work to meet the triple constraints.

---

[33] Cf. (Project Management Institute, 2004), p. 8 f.
[34] Cf. (Cleland & Ireland, 2006), p. 110
[35] Cf. (Phillips, 2010), p. 424
[36] Cf. (Dobson, 2004), p. 12

17

The project management life cycle is a collection of generally sequential project phases, also described as process groups with certain relationship to each other. A classic project management life cycle can be divided in five phases: initiating, planning, executing, controlling and lastly, the closing phase. The following illustration shows the project life cycle. Each phase has at least one connection to another project phase.

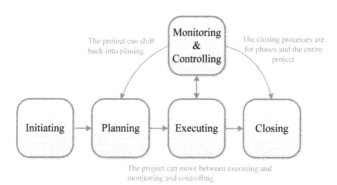

Figure 5: Project Lifecycle (PLC), based on Phillips, 2010, p. 3

3.2.1   Initiating

The project initiation process group is the launch of the project. Initiation is generally based on identified needs that justify the expense, risk, and allocation of resources for the project to exist.[37] Often the initiation is started by processes like program management or portfolio management, operative or strategic management or from somewhere else within an organisation. This fact may blur the project boundaries for the official initiation phase. During the initiation, preliminary project scope is developed and the project goal is defined. It is also important to show and prove that a specific project is the best alternative solution to satisfy the requirements.[38]

---

[37] Cf. (Phillips, 2010), p. 4
[38] Cf. (Project Management Institute, 2004), p. 43

3.2.2 Planning

The project planning process group develops the project management plan, as a first basis for the executing phase. The plan shows which processes will be used in the project, how the project work will be executed, how project work is to be controlled and how phases or milestones close down and the project ends.[39] The project management plan is actually a collection of smaller plans that address different areas of the project. This phase also identifies, defines and develops, the project scope, cost, resources and everything else that may occur within the project. For example, potential risks or issues, concerned stakeholders and reporting. Planning is an interactive process - every schedule deviation and activity delay during the project has to be rescheduled. The planning phase does not only take place at the beginning of a project, but indeed continuously to the end. [40]

3.2.3 Executing

This process group is about creating the operative product or service.. Executing involves performing the activities of the project in accordance with the project plan, as well as coordinating people and resources.[41] Project execution is unique to each discipline and is led and directed by the project manager. The project manager has to acquire, develop, manage and lead the project team to create the product or service the stakeholders are expecting.[42] Other important aspects during performing the activities of the project plan are quality assurance and procurement. Both have a high influence on the cost and therefore on budget. Variances during the execution may affect the project plan and require an analysis. The result can trigger a change request, regarding the project plan, which will be performed within the planning phase.

3.2.4 Monitoring and Controlling

This process group observes and measures the project performance regularly, to identify variances from the project management plan. The monitoring provides the project team

---

[39] Cf. (Phillips, 2010), p. 5
[40] Cf. (Project Management Institute, 2004), p. 46
[41] Cf. (Project Management Institute, 2004), p. 56
[42] Cf. (Phillips, 2010), p. 6

insight into the health of the project and directs additional attention to those areas that are in need. The monitoring and controlling phase also provides feedback between different project phases and implements corrective or preventive actions, when variances jeopardize the project objectives.[43] If problems, issues, or new risks occur, then the project shifts back to project planning, for revision or modification before moving back into execution. This process group also verifies that the project scope has met the stakeholder requirements so that the project deliverables are accepted. Regular recurring scope verification is a process that leads to acceptance decisions for the project.[44]

3.2.5   Closing

The closing process group includes all activities for terminating a project and hands off the completed outcome to others to close or cancel the project. Further it verifies that the defined processes are completed, and formally establishes that the project is finished. [45] This group does not only close the project as a whole, it also formally closes the other process groups, like executing and planning. Subsequent activities, like documenting lessons learned, post-delivery support, warranties, inspections, and regular payments are also part of the closing group.[46] During the closing the responsibility for the project`s outcome, like products, services or knowledge is often transferred to others.

3.3   Portfolio and program management

Large changes in organisation are nearly always performed within a project. Companies usually perform many projects, in various stages of development, concurrently. These projects often depend on each other and have direct or indirect technical or content driven relationships and compete with each other for resources.[47] Therefore, it is expedient to implement processes and structures that help to choose the appropriate projects in the correct priority, based on the business needs. One popular option to structure the multi

---

[43] Cf. (Project Management Institute, 2004), p. 59
[44] Cf. (Phillips, 2010), p. 7
[45] Cf. (Project Management Institute, 2004), p. 66
[46] Cf. (Phillips, 2010), p. 9
[47] Cf. (Pfetzing & Rohde, 2006), p. 69

project management is   project portfolio management, in combination with program management.

Related Projects are joined to a program in order to obtain benefits, by controlling and managing them as one and not individually. Programs and projects are input for the portfolio management. A portfolio is a collection of projects or programs and other work that is grouped together for effective management, to meet the strategic business objectives of an organisation. On the basis of different categories, like benefit/risk assessment and feasibility studies, funding and support can be assigned. The main goal of portfolio management is to balance between the investments for efficient use of resources and to maximise the value of the portfolio, by regular reviews and the strategic orientation of the organisation.[48] Additionally, the relationships and dependencies between projects and programs are considered and registered.

3.4   Characteristic of IT projects

IT projects do not differ from non-IT projects in their main characteristics like temporary, goal orientated and unique. Therefore, the same general project management methods can be applied to non IT projects and IT projects.[49] However, there are some particularities regarding IT in general and during some IT project phases.

3.4.1   Special characteristics of IT projects

One distinctive feature of IT projects are the invisibility and intangibility of its' services and products. Hardware, like server, router and user interface devices is tangible, but its' function can't be directly seen. Similarly, software is intangible and nearly invisible. Software is, all in all, a collection of text and documents like design documents, operation manuals and source code. None of them have any real significance for the user of the IT. The user often only sees a graphical user interface that represents the whole result of an IT

---

[48] Cf. (Project Management Institute, 2004), p. 17 ff.
[49] Cf. (Pfetzing & Rohde, 2006), p. 24

project.[50] This visualisation problem is a source of potential IT project failures. Even with tools for graphical representations, it is extremely challenging to represent the key facets of software in a way that is accessible to the project stakeholders. IT had has no physical restrictions, like buildings, bridges or ships. Therefore, the requestor asks for functions that are over-ambitious, or even impossible to deliver, without having any sense of the level of complexity entailed in meeting their request.[51] There is the tendency to include requirements that are desire desirable; rather than what is really needed because it is difficult to show the additional complexly. Another difficulty associated with the invisibility of IT projects, occurs during the monitoring phase. The lack of readily tangible products, means that a considerable time passes before problems become apparent. For significant quality testing, the product or service must be almost a final version.[52] Project controlling in IT projects are more time consuming and associated with more risks.

In addition to invisible and intangible IT, software workload especially, is difficult to measure. The software development process is creative one. There are many different ways to meet requirements, depending on the environment, the software framework and programming language and other conditions. Even experts in software often fail when it comes to estimating the line of code for the same piece of source code. Some of them would count the definition of variables or the inline developer comments, and some of them not. Estimates in a software project differ greatly for one person to from one person to another and it is hard to make useful experience in this area.[53] The difficulty is increased by the special complexity of IT projects.

Complexity is a significant obstacle to successful delivery of any project. Although major projects in other engineering disciplines are complex too, it seems that complexity in IT projects is both harder to detect and less understood.[54] A significant number of different

---

[50] Cf. (Suciu, 2013), p. 12
[51] Cf. (Royal Academy of Engineering and the British Computer Society, 2004), p. 14
[52] Cf. (Royal Academy of Engineering and the British Computer Society, 2004), p. 14
[53] Cf. (Suciu, 2013), p. 12
[54] Cf. (Royal Academy of Engineering and the British Computer Society, 2004), p. 15

levels between the electronic physical layer and the application layer, with various standard software elements like network protocols, directory services, authentication services and individual self-made software elements, like workflow source code or software interfaces, increases the complexity. All these factors are interwoven and have certain conditions that have to be considered. Another driver of complexity is the large number of transitions und translations between the life cycle phases of a product. The project goal is translated into business requirements, which is then translated into the functional specification. The functional specification is transformed into an analysis model, and so on. All these chains of translations makes the development process more vulnerable to errors.[55]

The majority of IT projects have an effect on operative business. Problems also commonly arise because the description of the business process does not accurately represent the process being employed. A good understanding of business and processes concerned with the IT project is necessary, even if the people involved have to alter their practices because of the project. Only requirements that support the project goal, should drive the complexity of a project. The remainder can interfere with the efficiency and reliability of the IT. The degree of complexity entailed in achieving a particular project objective, can be very difficult to estimate at the project beginning. A direct consequence of this aspect, is that projects may involve much more complexity than was originally realised.[56]

A related problem for IT projects is abuse of the perceived flexibility and the resulting dynamic of software. In classical engineering projects, like road building or shipbuilding, the project progress and the resulting restrictions are obvious. Because of the inability to visualise the boundaries of what is possible or practical in IT, people have a tendency to change their mind more frequently. Moreover, where people are accustomed to adapt their processes to suit a building, they will often request changes to software rather than modifying their own processes, because they think software is flexible.[57] Such "moving targets" for new features, or alternative functions during the course of the project, introduce

---

[55] Cf. (Suciu, 2013), p. 13
[56] Cf. (Royal Academy of Engineering and the British Computer Society, 2004), p. 15
[57] Cf. (Royal Academy of Engineering and the British Computer Society, 2004), p. 14

unnecessary complexity. Information technology is rapidly advancing; each year new standards and frameworks occur or disappear. The technology that was chosen at the project outset may no longer be supported or no longer matches with the IT strategy and is therefore replaced with another.[58]

Overall, IT projects suffer like any high tech project from high staff fluctuation, especially in countries with a lower wage level. Also, IT projects only create added value when they successfully finish. Partial results quickly become out-dated and are of little value for the organisation. The following table summarises the main characteristics of IT projects.

Characteristics	Driver
Invisible and intangible	- No physical restrictions - Hard to visualize - Time passes before problems become apparent - Complexity is hard to explain
Immeasurable	- Software development activity is creative - Hard to estimate line of code and therefore staff and resources
Complex	- Large number of levels between the physical layer and the digital layer - Several frameworks, standards and de facto standards - Transitions and translations between the life cycle phases - Understanding of business processes necessary
Dynamic	- No visual boundaries even when the project already at advanced stage - Request for changes, instead of modifying existing processes - Moving targets - Short product life cycles in IT

Table 1: Characteristics of IT projects, own illustration

3.4.2   Special characteristics within the project phases

There are several features during the executing and closing phase when dealing with IT projects. These features affect the development of IT, the testing and validation and the launch or go-live of IT projects. Some go-live activities can take place in the executing

---

[58] Cf. (Suciu, 2013), p. 13

phase and some activities may be a part of the closing phase. The following figure shows the special features during the executing and closing phase.

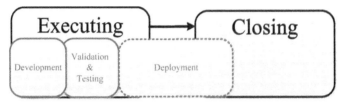

Figure 6: Special characteristics in IT projects, own illustration

Development

IT projects spend a lot of time in software development and systems integration. Computer systems are complex and combine different programming languages and self-develop systems with systems supplied by different software vendors. Within software development, a set of frameworks and approaches support the activities. These models and methodologies, also defined as Software Development Life Cycle (SDLC), have to be integrated into the project life-cycle, if used. SDLC, such as the Waterfall model, the Spiral model or agile software development, can be described along spectrum of agile, to iterative, to sequential. Depending on the IT Environment, the used programming language and other factors, the right SDLC method has to be chosen. The PLC is a generic approach that covers more than IT development. Even IT projects have to include things like business process changes, reorganization, marketing a new product/service and building a customer support structure, Thereby, the project life cycle encompasses all the activities of the project, while the software development life cycle focuses on realizing the product requirements.[59]

---

[59] Cf. (Taylor, 2003), p. 39

Testing and validation

One special challenge in IT projects, is to test the produced results as well as the transition to IT operations, including the go-live. No kind of IT and software is free of error. In fact, developers are unable to build defect-free software.[60] That's because of two main reasons. A first, developers are not able to test software under production conditions from the view of the .customer. Secondly, every Software has an infinite number of assumptions embedded in source code. The assumptions are not decisions that have been taken consciously; they arise from circumstances that were not thought about during the development process.[61] Therefore, the project deliverables have to be tested to get information about the quality of the software. The project results and the project objectives have to be compared as well. Testing needs a lot of time and resources. Every department and staff member that has to deal with the software in the future, should be involved in testing. Software testing is usually performed at different levels during the project and development process. The main levels are unit-, integration-, and system testing. Unit testing verifies the functioning in isolation of software pieces that are individually testable. Integration testing verifies the interaction between different software components and system testing is concerned with the behaviour of a whole system, including old and new software components. The last step is also known as the "user acceptance test". This test phase confirms that the software meets agreed-upon requirements.[62] Testing is a special part of every IT project, and requires substantial resources.

Deployment and launch

Software deployment is defined as the process of putting software solutions into use and ultimately driving business success.[63] Within the scope of deployment, one may find the development environment, testing and validation environment, and the live environment during the productive launch. Only after the implementation of the project results into the productive IT environment, the investment starts to bring value to the business. All

[60] Cf. (International Software Certification Board, 2006), p. 15
[61] Cf. (Royal Academy of Engineering and the British Computer Society, 2004), p. 16
[62] Cf. (IEEE Computer Society, 2004), p. 5-3
[63] Cf. (IBM Corporation, 2004), p. 1

preceding stages create only costs with little or no value for the business. In particular, the transition of software within client-server environments, presents many challenges. On the one side there are a relatively low number of big servers and databases that host the main application and on the other side, there are hundreds or hundreds of thousands of clients. These clients can be a simple application GUI like SAP or a browser for web shops like amazon.com. There are different ways to distribute software and hardware: The IT service is deployed initially, to a part of the user base, and this operation is repeated for the next part, until every client and server is updated.[64] The other way is to deploy the IT service in only one operation, to all clients and server. For changes that only consist of software deliverables, a push and pull approach is possible. The service is pushed out from a distribution server to the target location. Some deployment activities may require downtime and therefore an interruption of the affected business processes. To minimise the interruption of the IT service during the launch, is a major challenge for IT projects and IT operations.

4   Interfaces between IT operations and IT projects

The temporary and unique nature of projects, stands in contrast with IT operations that performs repetitive and permanent functional activities to deliver IT services. The management of these two systems is quite different, although they sometimes overlap and share some of the following characteristics:[65]

- Performed by people
- Constrained by limited resources
- Planned, executed, and controlled

The objectives of projects and operations are fundamentally different. A Project has to achieve its objectives and then terminate. The other way around the objective of on-going operations is to sustain the business. The difference is that the project concludes when its specific objectives have been achieved, while operations adopt and develop new objectives and the work continues. Because of the goal-oriented characteristic of projects, it may tend

---

[64] Cf. (The Stationery Office - B, 2011), p. 119
[65] Cf. (Project Management Institute, 2004), p. 6

27

to focus on one or a set of IT services, whereas IT operations tends to focus on delivering and supporting all IT services at the same time. IT operations perform ongoing, repeatable management processes and activities, with high priority for the day-to-day business. The result is that operational staff is often not available for project actives and cannot participate sufficiently in decisions. This leads to IT services which are difficult to operate, or which do not include adequate manageability functionality.[66] If nothing else has been agreed, the project staff may move on to the next project when finished and is not available to support difficulties in the operational environment. Projects are normally an undertaking outside of the normal operations of an entity; nevertheless projects can affect a few, or all levels of the organisation.[67]

The link between projects and IT operations is not only the simple handover and transition at the end of the project. In order to make the handover to the on-going operations without any complications and as frictionless as possible, the project and IT operations have to identify which additional transitional actions at the end of the project, are included or not included.[68] There are several actions during the project phases that have to be performed by IT operations as well, depending on the organizational structure. Some of these actions are absolutely necessary to ensure IT operations in a proper way and therefore obligatory in view of operations. Other activities can be performed in terms of a service for the project.

4.1   Organisational aspects

Projects are typically part of an organisation that is larger than the project. Even when the Project is external, it will be still influenced by the performing organization that initiated it. Most organizations have developed unique and describable cultures, reflected in factors like shared values, norms, view of authority relationships, policies and procedures. The company organisation often limits the available staff and other resources to the project. The place of the project within the organisation depends on the organisational structure that can

---

[66] Cf. (The Stationery Office - C, 2011), p. 234
[67] Cf. (Project Management Institute, 2004), p. 7
[68] Cf. (Project Management Institute, 2004), p. 23

differ in a spectrum from functional to projectized, with a variety of matrix structures in between.[69]

Project Characteristics	Organization Structure				
	Functional	Matrix			Projecttized
		Weak Matrix	Balanced Matrix	Strong Matrix	
Project Manager's Authority	Little or None	Limited	Low to Moderate	Moderate to High	High to Almost Total
Resource Availability	Little or None	Limited	Low to Moderate	Moderate to High	High to Almost Total
Who controls the project budget	Functional Manager	Functional Manager	Mixed	Project Manager	Project Manager
Project Manager's Role	Part-time	Part-time	Full-time	Full-time	Full-time
Project Management Staff	Part-time	Part-time	Part-time	Full-time	Full-time
Project Management Office	not existing	not existing	existing	existing	existing

Table 2: Organizational structures influences on projects, based on
Project Management Institute, 2004, p 28.

Communication between different units, if not covered by implemented processes, is passed up the organizational hierarchy to the department head, who consults with another department head. In contrast, the projectized organisation, the staff often belongs to one or more projects. A lot of the organization's resources are involved in project work, and project managers have a great deal of independence and authority. Other resources provide support services to various projects.[70] The influences of organizational structures on projects are shown in Table 2. Matrix organisations are a blend of functional and projectized characteristics, where the project has more or less considerable authority. This classification is largely theoretical, even a fundamentally functional organisation may create a special project team with full time staff and a project manager with considerable authority. But, a matrix organisation brings out the presence of conflicting project and

---

[69] Cf. (Project Management Institute, 2004), p. 28
[70] Cf. (Project Management Institute, 2004), p. 29

29

functional goals and objectives. If functional staff participates in projects, these resources have in fact two managers: the project manager to whom the employees report when they are assigned to a project, or when they perform a task for the project and the functional manager.[71] Any deviation from the project plan or other events, may cause resource constraints, and these conflicts often have to be resolved by the top management.

4.2   Transition processes

Due to the fact that changes are a part of normal business activates, there are several processes that supports the transition from IT projects to IT operations. These processes ensure that every IT project is developed and tested, with no exemptions from the agreed policies and frameworks. Processes also plan and conduct the deployment of the changes to the live environment while protecting the integrity of existing IT services. A key challenge to every transition process, is that many of its activities may already be underway with disparate agendas and authorities, like projects or business development units.

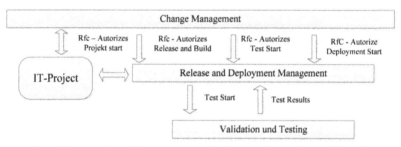

Figure 7: Example of transition process interaction, based on Kresse & Bause, 2008, p. 119

Figure 7 shows the possible interweaving of an IT project and transition processes. The shown change management process, as described in chapter 2.2.3, classically belongs to transition processes by theory. But it may be reasonable to perform the change management activities within IT operations. In particular, when many small operational requests for change need to be processed. The other transition processes may be integrated in different

---

[71] Cf. (Michael W. Newell, 2004), p. 9

departments within the organizational structure as well. For example: the release and deployment management process may be hosted by a project management office, if useful. According to requirements, the IT project has to trigger the processes early and proactively. The transition processes are available for the projects, but they would not observe all current projects, to offer them their service at the right time or to remind them that the processes need to be performed.

4.2.1 Transition planning and support

Projects tend to focus on their own transition goals, while IT operations focus on overall ongoing operations. The establishment of new or changed IT services into the productive environment is a critical part. If errors occur during this phase, an IT service may be unavailable for an extended time. The purpose of transition planning and support is to coordinate the resources that take part in transition activities and to provide overall planning for all transition tasks. In order to manage a large number of changes and projects, the process provides a collection of policies and frameworks for the transition phase and ensures that all parties adopt and accept this standard. Transition planning and support determine and define the operational tools that support the transition, like tools for testing activities and tools that plan deployment in detail. Identification, management and the control of risk across projects, is also part of transition planning and support.[72] For Example: transition planning and support may determine that only two major releases, go into the productive environment per year. The coordination of efforts to enable multiple transitions at the same time and the efforts to solve conflicts regarding resources, are of great added value to projects and business.

4.2.2 Release and deployment management

The purpose of the release and deployment management is to plan and control the test and deployment of authorized changes. This process ensures that the IT services work as intended, when the release is introduced into existing infrastructure. A release is defined as one or more approved changes that are built, tested and deployed together as a single entity.

---

[72] Cf. (The Stationery Office - B, 2011), p. 52 ff.

The build procedure includes a collection of developed or bought components with installation instructions and operation manual, packed as one unique bundle.[73] A release may include hardware, software, documentation, processes or other components.[74] Releases are often divided into:

- Major releases, generally containing significantly improved functionality, some of which may make intervening fixes to problems redundant. A major upgrade or release usually supersedes all preceding minor upgrades, releases and emergency fixes.

- Minor releases usually contain small enhancements and fixes, some of which may have already been issued as emergency fixes. A minor upgrade or release usually supersedes all preceding emergency fixes.

- Emergency fixes normally contain the corrections to a small number of known failures or problems[75]

Any distribution of a release bundle, including financial aspects like license and operational cost, belongs to this process area. More specifically, release and deployment management is responsible for defining and organizing the compatibility of deployments of changes intended to update or upgrade the production environment, so as to identify, manage and limit risks that could interrupt the IT service.[76] Actually, the process is responsible for planning, building, deployment and subsequent verification of the release in the appropriate IT environment. During the planning activities, a distinctive feature of release and deployment management, is the organization of multiple changes, possibly from multiple sources, into one timely release, appropriate for the business. The outcome of IT projects and other sources are merged to one release that is tested by the validation and testing process.[77] The first weeks after deployment to the live environment, the operational staff gets early life support (ESL) from resources that develop the IT service. During this time, a team consisting of development, operation and project members support the handover to IT

[73] Cf. (Ebel, 2008), p. 408
[74] Cf. (The Stationery Office, 2007), p. 243
[75] Cf. https://www.ucisa.ac.uk/~/media/
[76] Cf. http://www.ca.com/us/, p. 2
[77] Cf. http://www.ca.com/us/, p. 5

operation. ESL provides appropriate resources to resolve operational and support issues quickly (like incidents and hotfixes), centrally and locally. This ensures that the users can use the IT service without or with only some unwarranted disruption.[78]

4.2.3 Validation and testing

The purpose of the validation and testing process, is to provide quality assurance that the new or changed service delivered, satisfies the customer requirements. The performed test helps to identify errors and bugs in the IT service, created or modified before the IT service is released to live environment. Found bugs go back to the project in order to fix it. Poor testing may result in an increasing number of service desk calls, incidents, problems and errors. The cost of fixing bugs and errors post deployment, is far greater than fixing them during testing. IT services with failures and errors, may not be used effectively by the user to deliver the desired value and can therefore result in serious conflicts between IT operations and non IT departments.[79] A well-defined service validation and testing process consists of the following activities:

- Test management: This consists of identifying issues and risks, managing and controlling the activities that have taken place during all test phases, to ensure that the release is fit for use.

- Test Planning: Developing a test plan that would act as an input to testing. This includes resources, supporting services, scheduling milestones for delivery and acceptance.

- Verification of test plans and test design: Ensures that the test design and test plan is complete and accurate. Plans and designs are validated to ensure all activities are complete and that the required resources are available.

- Prepare test environment: Create a test environment that is similar to the live environment. This includes the necessary access for the test staff, the data that is needed to conduct the test and the test cases it needs to perform.

---

[78] Cf. (The Stationery Office - B, 2011), p. 143
[79] Cf. (The Stationery Office - B, 2011), p. 150

- Testing: Conduct testing by using manual or automated testing techniques and procedures. All results are recorded during the Test. The issues and errors found are also recorded.

- Evaluate: Compare the actual results with the projected results. Evaluate exit criteria, and reports

- Clean up and closure: Ensure that the test environment is cleaned. Learn from previous experiences and identify areas for improvement.[80]

The target group of the validation and testing process are end users, service owners and IT operations, who are responsible for the service after the transition. Operational test cases should include the normal day to day business like installation and starting the IT service, as well as incident handling, by producing an error proactive in the test environment. Test automation may create a great value for the process, by increasing speed and reliability of testing. Several test environments for system-, integration- and user acceptance tests, avoid resource conflicts. Organisations with different test environments are able to test in parallel if useful, and maintain more than one release at the same time.

4.3   IT operations activities during the project life cycle

The mentioned processes from chapter 4.2 support the project transition to operations. Process managers are able to manage and control their processes, but they are not capable of performing every activity to finish the process by themselves. For example: The installation of software within a certain environment, requires the special skills of IT operations staff. The release and deployment management process, therefore depends on these available resources. Transition process supports IT operations in such complex and time consuming activities, like planning, analysis, coordination and communication - but many tasks have to be practically carried out by IT operations staff.

In a classical approach, the main activity of transitions processes starts at the end of a project. But, project phases like initiating, planning and executing are also included in

---

[80] Cf. http://manage-it.biz/service-validation-and-testing/

transition processes, as shown in Figure 8. The following part shows additional connections between IT operations, and the project phases. Some activities are obligatory for IT operations to ensure stable and reliable day-to-day operation, others are optional.

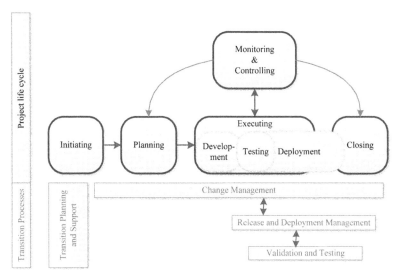

Figure 8: Project life cycle and transition processes, own illustration

4.3.1   Initiating

The preparation of the first project idea needs a lot of reliable data in practice. The starting point of IT operations needs to be defined, if the goal of the project has to be measurable and relevant. IT operations may consult projects during the initiating phase in terms of technology, operating costs and present baseline.[81]

Other consulting activities may contain infrastructure design, selection of software like OS and Database type and in some cases programing. The operational staff knows best, what is possible in the existing IT environment, and what kind of solution can be supported by existing resources in the best way. In exceptional cases, the operations staff may conduct

---

[81] Cf. (Ebel, 2008), p. 548

35

atypical activities, like business process design or end-to-end test of business processes. These kinds of consulting activities are a special working relationship between IT operations and IT project. The employee joins the project for these activities and works under the authority of the project manager. This kind of headcount leasing is the basis for every matrix organisation and needs an agreement between project and operations. If agreed, the operational staff may join the project in every phase for a certain set of activities.[82]

Quite often projects may be also initiated by IT operations itself. The modifying of a software system after delivery to correct faults, improve performance or other attributes belongs to maintenance activities.[83] The initiation of maintenance projects with the objective to stay in manufacturer support, normally is the responsibility of IT operations. Without manufacturer support the established SLA cannot be guaranteed. The scope of such projects may include hardware and network components, new or upgraded system software, like operating systems and middleware etc. and new or upgraded application software.[84]

4.3.2   Planning

During the planning phase certain actions must be performed by IT operations that are in their own interests. IT operations formulate a set of non-functional requirements, to ensure that the project deliverables can operate in the desired fashion. Non-functional requirements define the overall qualities or attributes of the resulting IT service. These kinds of requirements, place restrictions and specify external constraints on the IT service that must be considered during the design and development.[85] These requirements concern every operation aspect of the IT service life cycle. Table 3 shows an overview of the most common operational requirements category groups.

---

[82] Cf. (The Stationery Office - C, 2011), p. 228
[83] Cf. http://dis.unal.edu.co/~icasta/
[84] Cf. (The Stationery Office - C, 2011), p. 228
[85] Cf. http://www.iai.uni-bonn.de/III/

When the IT project deliverables reach the live environment, the IT services have to be "supportable" into the future? The IT services have to be capable of being supported from a technical viewpoint, within existing or planed resources and staff skills. IT operations has to take care that there are no complex support paths between multiple supports departments of third-party organisations and that there is no adverse impact on existing technical or operational working practices, processes or schedules.[86]

Additionally, the effect of the IT projects has to be evaluated. The effects of changes during the project and after the launch of the project results must be analysed systematically from the view of IT operations. This analysis contains the ability to model the effect of changes and a detailed resource plan for all project activities and activities that will be necessary after the project.[87] Deeper analysis is intended to find tasks and actives that are not considered by the project plan, but needed to accomplish the project goals. This kind of hidden expenditure often causes a conflict between IT project and IT operations, regarding staff and other resources. For this purpose, every relevant project output during the planning phase has to be reviewed and approved by operation. These may include requirement specifications, system specification and design, architectural concepts and so on. The change management process supports the formal release for these kinds of project documents.

Some operational services can be offered as an option for the project. If agreed, IT operation may provide staff or other resources for dedicated project tasks. These characteristics, length and the objective of such kind of body leasing, have to be recorded between project and operation. In general, the nature of tasks should match with the skills of the IT staff. It may not be efficient, if a database expert would take responsibility for the quality of java source code within a project. The task should not be formulated as an IT task in general, it has to be a specific project task for a specific expert team.

---

[86] Cf. (The Stationery Office - C, 2011), p. 228
[87] Cf. (The Stationery Office - C, 2011), p. 48

Non-functional Requirements	Description
Capacity & Scalability Requirements	Capability & scalability requirements describe what kind of technical load the IT service has to design, and how to increase total output under an increased load, when resources (typically hardware) are added or increased.
Security Requirements	Security requirements are included in an IT service, to ensure the authorized access to the IT service and integrity of the IT service from accidental or malicious damage.
Maintainability & Supportability Requirements	Supportability requirements are concerned with the ease of changes to the system after deployment. Supportability is the ability to change the system, to deal with additional application modifications, like new technology, defect fixes, international conventions, etc.
Availability & Reliability Requirements	Reliability requirements describe the ability of a system to perform its required functions, under stated conditions, for a specific period of time. Availability describe the degree to which a system or component is operational and accessible when required for use. Availability is often expressed as a probability.
Performance Requirements	Performance requirements are concerned with the timing characteristics of an IT service. This includes speed, efficiency, resource consumption, throughput, and response. Certain tasks or features are more time-sensitive than others; the nonfunctional requirements should identify those IT service functions that have constraints on their performance.
Interface & Interoperability Requirements	Interface & interoperability requirements describe how the IT service is to interface with the environment, users and other systems. Polly designed interfaces are prone to interference.

Table 3: Categories of non-functional Requirements, based on
http://dis.unal.edu.co/~icasta/ and http://www.iai.uni-bonn.de/III/

4.3.3   Executing

In context of development, IT operations have to review and approve every change and modification of the project scope. Changes during the project execution are mostly short-term and urgent, but may contain restrictions or additional efforts. This project modification has to be approved by the change management process implicitly, to avoid handling with lack of attention. If parties have agreed that the development environment will be operated by IT operations, they should make a special SLA for this kind of operation. Even when the main focus of every IT Operation is the live environment, a project also needs reliable availability.

The non-functional requirement that has been recorded in the project specifications has to be validated by operational staff, during the test part in the executing phase. Occurring errors or deviations, go back to development, in order to fix them. Before the test starts, every participant has to be trained in handling the IT service, to ensure that a feature is not confused with a real error. The test cases should also be developed by the staff that is responsible for the IT service in live environment.[88] The test case creation and performing is supervised by validation and testing process. Processes and working procedures may need to be adapted to operate the new release in a suitable way. This adjustment has to be tested like the IT system as well. Tools that support the Incident- problem and event management process, need to be configured as well as technical aspects like monitoring systems, overall system access and so on. All accumulated knowledge should be transferred into a knowledge management system or database at the end of the test part.[89]

IT operations can optionally provide other services in the test phase. These services should be selected carefully, due to the fact that they may require a lot of resources. There is a high risk that the needed resources are underestimated because of the fact that projects are unique and the operating staffs has little experience with the new release. Included are, for instance: building the release, operating the test environment, initial release installation, installation of fixes, and so on. In particular, the determination of responsibility for the test environments must be one of the top priorities - this task may easily double the effort of IT operations.

In order to ensure a failure-free commissioning at the end of the IT project, the live environment should be quarantined for a specific time. During this time, no major changes

---

[88] Cf. (The Stationery Office - C, 2011), p. 46
[89] Cf. (The Stationery Office - B, 2011), p. 185

should be implement that may have an impact on the upcoming release. Such procedure guarantees that the live environment operates error-free, that no risky change is implemented and that the staff gets a short resting phase to focus on the upcoming challenge. The conditions, length and the date have to be defined by IT operations, in cooperation with release and deployment management. Before the launch starts, the deployment plan has to be reviewed. Ideally, the whole procedure is tested by a final rehearsal performed by IT operations staff. This approach offers two crucial benefits. The deployment plan is put to the acid test by operations and the performing staff gets a final training on handling with the new IT services. Nevertheless, in practice, the launch should always be supported by the project team. The rehearsal, launch and formal acceptance of all launch documents, needs to be authorised by the change management process. The responsibility for all deployment activities lies formally with release and deployment management. This may cause a classic resource conflict, if the IT operations staff performs the transition to the live environment. The functional operations manager needs to assign a part of his team for a specific set of tasks, to the release and deployment management process. If there is no precise agreement between the process managers and the functional managers, problems will definitely arise.

4.3.4 Monitoring and Controlling

Within the monitoring and controlling phase, IT operations focus on supporting the quality assurance. Assumptions that were made at the project launch, should be reviewed and revised regularly by the project team. Key estimates and assumptions relating to IT operations, should be checked by IT operations. In particular, this applies to future personnel expenses, budget, support contracts, software licenses and planned maintenance intervals. With regard to risk management all listed risks shall checked for operational impact. Risks associated with IT operations must be monitored to ensure correct classification and priority.

4.3.5 Closing

At the end of the project the complete responsibility for the IT service passes into IT operations. For this initial period, IT operations gets support from project members and developers within Early Life Support. The entry and exit criteria and other general conditions for the ESL should be matched with IT operations. At the end of the ELS the IT service runs on agreed SLA.[90]

Sometimes, projects are launched into the live environment even when some failures are not fixed. Often the project has no more time or budget to fix those errors. Nevertheless, if the launch is decided, all identified errors must be handed over to IT operations. Those known errors have to be registered to document root causes and workarounds. This exercise prevents unnecessary user requests and allows a quick diagnostic.[91]

The same procedure can be used by other incomplete project tasks or requirements, if agreed. For example: The creation of requested table views for an accounting system cannot be accomplished by the project, due to budget or time gap. The views can be created only by configuring the accounting system. To launch the software in time IT operation can configure, test and deploy the views into the live environment.

Once the project is launched, the software and hardware should be directly considered for maintenance planning. IT operation is responsible that the used hardware and software stays in manufacturer support. When the end of the manufacturer support becomes known, action needs to be taken. Either the IT service is replaced by another or gets an upgrade. In some cases, individual support contracts with suppliers are possible. It is conceivable that IT service runs without further manufacturer support and the SLA must be adjusted. When every activity is completed, a "lesson learned" workshop should be conducted as well. The results are useful to improve processes and organisation.

---

[90] Cf. (The Stationery Office - B, 2011), p. 143
[91] Cf. (Ebel, 2008), p. 491

41

5   Conclusion and further considerations

As outlined in the previous section, the relations and interfaces between IT projects and IT operations are various, not only limited to handover at the end of the project. Transitions processes, like release and deployment management, formally support the transfer to the live environment. On closer inspection, the transition processes support the transition with organisation and management, but the operational staff generates a large part of value added, mostly. For example: The deployment of software to the test environment is authorised by the change management process and organized by the release and deployment management. The execution of the installation requires expert staff for the installation, configuration, starting the software and performing the first operational validation before the environment can be used for testing activities.

This multiple use of IT operations may lead to a non-transparent resources allocation. Managers need to be aware of the fact that a lot of operational work is hidden behind these processes and that there is no unlimited performance available. Figure 9 shows possible relations between processes, project and IT operations. Transition processes and IT projects requires resources from IT operations. The processes have demands on particular results that, helps to produce the process outcome, like installation of a software packet for the release and deployment process. IT projects require various services, like operating the development environment, creating test data for a user acceptant test or other consulting activities. Participation from IT operations has to be performed during the entire project. A holistic approach to integrate project from an operational view may be the "Operational IT implementation management".

42

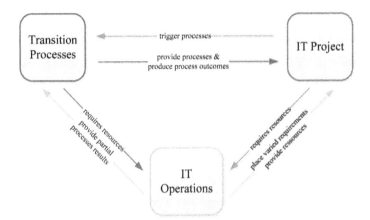

Figure 9: Connection between IT project, IT operations and transition processes, own illustration

With this approach, projects are an inherent part of IT operations from the beginning. All necessary operations activates, including activities that performed as a service and consulting activity, are transparent listed and planned along the project phases. To reduce overlapping of activities and resources, the process activities are included as well. The Appendix shows a matrix based on different tasks and activities with temporal assignment to the project phases. The separation between obligate activities and optional activities, shows clearly which kinds of tasks are handled by IT operations self-sufficiently and which tasks need to be agreed as headcount leasing or as a service for processes. This ensures transparency of key processes and the definition of tasks and responsibilities. For instance, the operation of the development environment during the execution phase, should be requested by the IT project and confirmed by IT operations.

On the one side IT operations is the keeper of status quo, but on the other side, a large amount of changes due to maintenance reasons have to be made to maintain this status quo. Changes to the IT environment are a permanent part of the work of IT operations. IT projects, regarded as an integral part of IT operations, offers a strong basis for business success.

List of Literature

- Bock, I. (2010). Optimierung von IT-Service-Organisationen. Münschen, DE: dpunkt Verlag.
- Cleland, D. L., & Ireland, L. R. (2006). PROJECT MANAGEMENT: Strategic Design and Implementation. McGraw-Hill Osborne Media.
- Dobson, M. S. (2004). The Triple Constraints in Project Management. Betheda, Maryland: Management Concepts.
- Ebel, N. (2008). ITIL V3 Basiswissen. Münschen, DE: Addision Wesley.
- IBM Corporation. (2004). The Software Deployment Mystery - Solved (Third Edition Ausg.). Rochester, Minnesota: BM Redbook.
- IEEE Computer Society. (2004). Guide to the Software Engineering Body of Knowledge. Los Alamito, USA: Institute of Electrical and Electronics Engineers.
- International Software Certification Board. (2006). Guide to the CSTE common body of knowledge. Orlando, USA: International Software Certification Board.
- itSMF International. Frameworks for IT Management. Amersfoort, NL: Van Haren Publishing.
- Kresse, M., & Bause, M. (2008). Learn ITIL v3. Bad Homburg, Deutschland: Serview GmbH.
- Michael W. Newell, M. N. (2004). The Project Management Question and Answer Book. New York: AMACOM.
- Pfetzing, K., & Rohde, A. (2006). Ganzheitliches Projektmanagement (Second edition Ausg.). Zürich: Versus Verlag.
- Phillips, J. (2010). IT Project Management (Third Edition Ausg.). Chicago, USA.
- pma PROJEKT MANAGEMENT AUSTRIA. (2009). IPMA Competence Baseline (Version 3.0 Ausg.). Wien, Austria.
- Project Management Institute. (2004). A Guide to the Project Management Body of Knowledge (Third Edition Ausg.). (P. M. Institute, Hrsg.) Newtown Square, USA.

- Royal Academy of Engineering and the British Computer Society. (2004). The Challenges of Complex IT Projects. Great Britain: Royal Academy of Engineering.
- Suciu, D. (03 2013). The features of IT Projects. TSM Today Software Magazine (8/2013), S. 11-13.
- Taylor, J. (2003). Managing Information Technology Projects. New York, USA: AMACOM Books.
- The Stationery Office - A. (2011). Service Design. London, UK.
- The Stationery Office - B. (2011). Service Transition. London, UK.
- The Stationery Office - C. (2011). Service Operation. London, UK.
- The Stationery Office. (2007). Service Operation. Norwich: Office of Goverment Commerce.

List of Internet Sources

1. http://dis.unal.edu.co/~icasta/GGP/_Ver_2012_1/Documentos/Normas/610-12-1990.pdf, 16.11.2013
2. http://manage-it.biz/service-validation-and-testing/, 15.11.2013
3. http://omtco.eu/wp-content/uploads/OMTCO-IT-Costs-The-Costs-Growth-And-Financial-Risk-Of-Software-Assets.pdf, 10.12.2013
4. http://www.ca.com/us/~/media/files/technologybriefs/33819-rel-depl-mgmt-tech-brf-final-7-27_213722.aspx, 20.11.2013
5. http://www.iai.uni-bonn.de/III/lehre/vorlesungen/SWT/RE05/slides/09_Non-functional%20Requirements.pdf, 30.10.2013
6. http://www.teamquest.com/pdfs/whitepaper/forrester-it-efficiency.pdf, 10.01.2014
7. https://oxforddictionaries.com/definition/english/project, 09.12.2013
8. https://www.ucisa.ac.uk/~/media/Files/members/activities/ITIL/servicetransition/release_deployment/ITIL_a%20guide%20to%20release%20and%20deployment%20mgmt%20pdf, 12.01.2014